MY JOURNEY WITH MY AUTISTIC SON

A Guide For Parents With Children With An IEP and 504 Plan

BY

DR. F. A. FULKS

Printed in the United States of America

First Edition, 2022

HARDBACK ISBN 978-1-0879-7779-9

EBOOK ISBN 978-1-0879-7890-1

Red Pen Edits and Consulting, LLC

P. O. Box 25283

Columbia, SC 29223

www.redpeneditsllc.com

Table of Contents

Dedications

First and foremost, this book is dedicated to the head of my life, God. I could not have made it through the storms of this journey without Him.

I also would like to thank
Diane C. Gaines (Co-Founder of Elvan's LifeLine),
Richard Handy,
Keith Alexander,
Stephen Gilchrist,
Raquel Jones,
Julie Mason Sheehan,
Precious Gilliam,
Dr. Katina Davis,
Lorene Riley,
Julie Syphertt,
Imani M. Hanley,
Dr. Tracy L. Haigler,
Leah Cherney,
Elvan Hanley,
and last, but certainly not least, my mother in Heaven,
Mary A. Riley.

To all of you who prayed for my son, encouraged him and believed in him,
Thank you.

Introduction

Mothers have an inept ability and connection with their children. From the moment's notice of pregnancy, the mother's heart is turned towards the child in such an undeniable manner. The child, although inside of the womb, can sense this love and affection and the connection is strength by months of development. After delivery, all babies need time to connect with the mother and father by laying on their chest as a point of connection and synchronization. All of these moments were shared with my son. From the beginning, I knew that my son was different and I knew that the pregnancy, in and of itself, was just as different. From day one of my child's life, there were complications, but he proved himself to be a fighter by defying death on multiple occasions. My son is a fighter. After a few short years, he dispelled rumors and misdiagnosis to overcome statistics and ultimately be victorious in the face of naysayers. My son is a fighter.

Most championship boxing matches are scheduled for 12 rounds, but they tend to end in less than that time expectancy. 12 is the number of establishment. If you look at the 12 years of my son's educational career, he had to endure numerous bouts in the classroom. From being picked on to being bullied, he always came out with the victory. On the other side, I, as the parent, also endured 12 long years of fighting. None of my battles were physical, but I had to extend my voice to speak on behalf of my son in a system that was not built in his favor.

In this book, you will hear of my son's journey from birth to current day. I don't want to tell the end from the beginning in this introduction, but you must understand that I am here and my son is here on purpose. As you read these chapters, I hope that my journey is positively influential for multiple reasons. First, I want every parent of a disabled child to acquire an IEP/504 plan for their educational success. Second, if you have an IEP/504 plan, I want to encourage every parent with a disabled child to understand and implement the plan to the fullest of their God-given rights. Next, I want every parent of a disabled child to start or continue being the voice of their child. You know what is best for your child. Lastly, if you know someone that has a disabled child with or without an IEP/504, to share this book with them. Ultimately, I want to educate parents on the proper methods to uphold their child's IEP/504 plan and position their child for success while in school and as they grow into adults.

This is my account of the journey with my successful autistic son.

CHAPTER ONE

Meet Elvan

1

Meet Elvan

My name is Dr. Florene Fulks. I am a life coach, licensed counselor, Pastor, wife and most importantly, a mother. I am honored to be the mother to two wonderful children, Imani Mahalia and Elvan. My son, Elvan, was diagnosed at an early age with having autism. Autism is a condition related to brain development that impacts how a person perceives and socializes with others, causing problems in social interaction and communication (Mayo Clinic). I want to start this book by describing my pregnancy. I almost had a normal pregnancy with Elvan. There were a few exceptions. Around the sixth or seventh month of my pregnancy, Elvan started standing up straight. I could see the print of his head on my belly. He just started straight up and I couldn't figure out for the life of me why he was stretched out like that. Little did I know, while in my belly, he was having grand mal seizures.

Hint, Hint

In this book, I hope to educate you on various terms and methodologies my process. Prepare to see these blocked off areas where definitions and further explanations will be provided to assist you, the reader, with gaining clarity and a deeper understanding.

Grand Mal Seizures are caused by abnormal electrical activity throughout the brain. A grand mal seizure causes a loss of consciousness and violent muscle contractions. It's the type of seizure most people picture when they think about seizures.
Mayo Clinic

I had no clue what grand mal seizures were. All I knew was that I couldn't move when he was standing and stretching straight up. Then, my body would relax in my belly, and he would go back to the normal fetal position. This was around the 6 or 7 month mark. Elvan was due in September, but in his own unpredictable manner, he decided that he was going to come early. We're almost at eight months and here comes Elvan. My water broke and I went directly to the hospital. My doctor said that his feet were coming first which meant that Elvan was breached which is not the recommended position to deliver. I was given some medicine that would cause Elvan to turn in my belly for a more traditional birthing. I don't know the name of the medication, but they gave me a shot in my hip to cause the turn. Well, that didn't work. Elvan was determined to come feet first. I was taken back to the delivery room for an emergency C-section.

The early days of my pregnancy was a very trying period of my life. My daughter was a normal pregnancy. She was healthy and did well. Two years later, I got pregnant with Elvan. My husband at the time and I were not on good terms. It is imperative for women that are pregnant to surround themselves with positive energy and a positive environment. Ultimately, it affects the unborn child. When my water broke signifying the entrance of Elvan into the world, I was very nervous. My maternal instincts are real and I knew something was wrong with this child. After being told that Elvan was trying to come out feet first, taking medication to get him to turn, and then having a C-section, Elvan arrived as a beautiful 7lb, 11oz baby boy. He was a beautiful baby with beautiful black hair. I was so happy to have a son.

The next day, my doctor notified me that Elvan experienced jaundice. Infant jaundice is yellow discoloration of a newborn baby's skin and eyes. For a few days, Elvan was kept under observation in the neonatal care unit. After about five days, I was able to take my son home. When we got home, everything was normal. He cried like a normal baby, and everything was fine. On the third day, I was combing my hair. I could see Elvan in the mirror as he lied on the bed. Suddenly, his body began convulsing. He was having grand mal epileptic seizures right in front of me. I immediately called 911 and he was rushed to the hospital. The seizures stopped temporarily, but after about 30 minutes, he had another seizure and coded, meaning he died.

You may need to read that again. Let's recap.

I just had a baby that had grand mal seizures in my womb. After five days in the neonatal care and three days home, he had another series of seizures and coded.....died at the hospital.

Ok. I just wanted to give you a brief overview of the first half of the first chapter of this journey.

The hospital staff asked me what I wanted to do. Without reservation or hesitance, I said, "RESUSCITATE!"

They put the infant-sized defibrillator on Elvan's chest and I could see his little body lift up off the table as they attempted to shock life back into my baby's body. They began to bring my son back as a result of the seizure. I don't know why he was having seizures, but they kept us in the hospital for two days for more observations. I left with a medicine called Phenobarbital to control Elvan's seizures. His dosage required one in the morning and one at night. I didn't like the medicine because it would make his eyes roll in the back of his head. The doctor said that if he didn't take this medicine, he would seizure to death. The seizures did slow down.

That wasn't the only time that Elvan died. The second time he had a seizure at about five months old. I took him to the hospital and he died at Harlem Hospital. They resuscitated him again. The last time, my husband at the time and I were in St. George, South Carolina, visiting my mother. I knew something was going to happen. Remember, my maternal instincts never fail me. Elvan was about 10 months old. He had a fever and all of the stores were closed. I just wanted to get some baby Tylenol to bring down the fever. In the meantime, I used a cool rag on him. Around 2:30am, he started having a seizure. I ran down the hallway to get my mom. By the time I came back, my husband, Elvan P. Hanley, had his limp body in his hands and said, "He's gone, Florene."

I yelled to the top of my lungs, "Bring him back! Bring him back!" I will never forget this. My husband put his mouth over Elvan's mouth while covering his nose started breathing into him frantically. All of a sudden, I saw my son jump. He brought him back. To this day, I tell my now ex-husband that because of him, my son lived. There is no way that I would have been able to do that.

In the 11th month, we experienced a miracle. God visited me and told me to anoint my son from head to toe. Out of obedience, I did what God said and I could feel a sensation like hot water was pouring on me. I knew at that moment that I was in the midst of a miracle. From that moment, God told me that Elvan was healed of grand mal seizures.

I took Elvan back to the hospital and asked the doctor to do another EKG and other tests on Elvan's brain to gauge the seizure activity. After the doctors performed the test, they responded in an angry yet confused tone. They accused me of not bringing the same back to the hospital. Why in the world would I bring another baby in for testing and where would I get that baby from?

"Ma'am! You didn't bring the same baby in here. This isn't Elvan's brain.", said the doctor.
"Yes it is!", I responded.

The doctors went on to explain that it was impossible based on the results from the CT scans and EKG tests on his brain. "This is not the same brain", said the confused doctors. The doctors mentioned that the scans looked as if someone blew the seizure activity out of Elvan. Because of this, it was recommended by the doctors that Elvan be taken off Phenobarbital. Within the first month, he was weaned off of the medicine. Elvan was healed and he never had a grand mal seizure again. Never! That was a miracle!

I know Elvan is a miracle child. Dr. Charles Nichter from the St. Luke's Hospital in New York City deemed Elvan a miracle child. Dr. Nichter was a neonatal doctor that specialized in babies that had seizures and other health complications. Even with the miracles, there were residual effects. I had to deal with these after effects and this after effect came in the form of autism. This shook me to my core for two reasons. First of all, I didn't know what autism was. Secondly, once you have autism, you always have it. That's complicated for me as a person of faith. I don't believe that you have to have autism forever because God can do anything. I had no clue of the challenges I would have to face with a son with autism.

During grand mal seizures, and most seizures for that matter, there is a loss of oxygen to the brain. This loss of oxygen can cause traumatic damage to the brain. Elvan had many seizures. I noticed around the age of 1 and a half to two years old, that Elvan was a very floppy baby. Meaning, he was almost like jelly. He also wasn't functioning and thriving like my daughter, Imani. I gathered that the seizures had an adverse effect on his motor skills. For a period of time, he wouldn't track items with his eyes. It wasn't until he was about four years old that he started doing better. Even then, there was no language. Elvan could not speak. He would only sound out single syllable words. My daughter was speaking in complete sentences at the age of 18 months old.

We decided to put Elvan into a highly recommended and reputable daycare. During the summer, the director advised me that Elvan couldn't come back to the daycare. I wondered what my son had done wrong. She said that Elvan wasn't acclimating well to his surroundings. When they would have group activities, Elvan would walk away, lay on the floor and put his ear to the floor as if he was hearing sounds or noises. During arts and crafts, Elvan would say that he couldn't do finger painting because the paint hurt his hands which caused him to cry endlessly. Elvan was very sensitive. When I say sensitive, I'm talking about him being sensitive to the touch. He did not like certain things to touch him like rice. He didn't like for his foot to touch the grass. During learning activities, Elvan did not like for anyone to sit next to him. He would walk off and sit by himself. These were just a few of the observations made by the director of the daycare. She felt bad taking my money without Elvan experiencing the full educational opportunities that the daycare offered. "If you want to keep him here, that's fine with me. However, I think something is wrong." I didn't know what "something" meant.

When Elvan turned five years old, I took him to another sought after daycare named Hannah's Learning Lab. I will never forget this learning center. I told the African-American director of this daycare what the previous daycare said to me and I was immediately questioned in this manner: "Is he retarded?"

I did not like that and I responded with an emphatic, "No!"

She responded, "Well, I'll be the judge of that and if he is retarded, I will let you know." She accepted Elvan into her program. I was so happy that someone accepted my son. Within three weeks, Elvan learned how to spell him name. Mind you, he wasn't learning or thriving at the other daycare. He was able to spell his entire name at this new daycare – Elvan Akeem Hanley. Over the next six months, Elvan knew his name, how to recognize words, and knew colors in English and Spanish. Not only did he recognize colors in Spanish, he knew how to spell colors in Spanish. The director scheduled a meeting with me to advise me that there is nothing wrong with my son. My son just learned differently. This taught me that with the right amount of patience and care, learning is the inevitable.

Those were the daycare years. I observed Elvan's interactions with other children. There is one incident that stands out to me. While Elvan played with his cousins, he would be running around and crying. Running and crying. I wondered what was wrong with him so I asked him what was the matter. Elvan said, "Mr. Sun won't leave me alone." Elvan thought that the sun was following him around. This is another indicator of how sensitive he was to touch and feelings. I had to let Elvan know that the sun was in the sky and that during the summertime, the sun is always shining down. That's how Elvan learned differently, but I thought that was the cutest expression about dealing with the sun.

Next, was the first grade. Elvan wasn't sick. Like I previously stated, he didn't have any more seizures. I allowed Elvan to stay in the daycare with Miss Hanna until the age of seven. However, I knew that I had to remove him from that daycare and get him into elementary school. Elvan entered the first grade at the age of seven. I figured that would give him a head start. He'll almost be like the other children at the same age. This first grade teacher said, "something is wrong with him." The school diagnosed Elvan with Attention-deficit/hyperactivity disorder (ADHD).

Attention-deficit/hyperactivity disorder (ADHD) is a chronic condition that affects millions of children and often continues into adulthood. ADHD includes a combination of persistent problems, such as difficulty sustaining attention, hyperactivity and impulsive behavior.

Mayo Clinic

Elvan was easily distracted and not focused like the other children, but he was smart. The school advised me to have him placed on a medication called, Focalin 5mg. That helped him focus better, but it took his appetite. Throughout the first and second grade, Elvan consistently passed all of his classes and made above an 86 average. All the school could say was that he was different.

One thing I learned about Elvan was that he was a very affectionate person. While living in New York, I learned from an African doctor at the Harlem Hospital that Elvan was going to be a loving baby. He said that when Elvan was born that he needed to feel safe. That made me spoil Elvan even more. I wanted him near me. Close to me. Hugging me. Elvan always loved affection. He loves affection and he loves praise.

"Elvan, you did a wonderful job!"

"Elvan, I can't believe you got all of them right. Great job!"

"Elvan, you are the greatest!"

That's the kind of accolades and praise that he needed. On the other hand, my daughter was different. "Imani, that was good." She was fine with that. Elvan needed more praise. More hugs. More attention.

That's the synopsis of Elvan's first and second grade school years. I had no problems with the schoool. I had no problems with the teachers. They all accepted Elvan. They accepted his ADHD and I did too, because that's the diagnosis that I was told.

Then, the third grade came and that's where the war began. This is where my battles started in Columbia, South Carolina. Elvan went into regular third grade classes, but one of the teachers, once again, mentioned that Elvan was different. They didn't acknowledge his learning as being ADHD. The district psychologist contacted me to meet then at a middle school to have Elvan tested. They tested Elvan for almost 20-25 minutes. When the results came back, they sent me a letter with a diagnosis saying that Elvan was borderline mentally retarded. Based on this diagnosis, school district was required to place Elvan in a self-contained learning classroom. This is also known as special education.

I learned at Miss Hanna's Learning Center that Elvan was neither mentally retarded, profoundly retarded nor borderline retarded. I knew Elvan was different, but I did not know what the difference was. I told the district psychologist that I was not going to receive that. I needed help to understand. What is a self-contained learning class? I was told that it was the same as a regular classroom, but the teacher taught at a slower pace. They learn the same stuff, but a slower pace. That's what I was told. They removed Elvan from the regular class, and ultimately that school, to be placed in another school in a self-contained learning class. So, my life and normalcy were turned upside down. I had to drive away from the school that my son was zoned for, to another school.

Elvan has always been inquisitive. He wanted to know why he was going to a new school. I had to make sure that he was comfortable with the new school and making new friends. The main thing that Elvan couldn't understand was why the other kids' parents weren't in the class every day, all day, like me. As much as Elvan was curious, I was even more curious. I wanted to know what this self-contained classroom experience was all about. I took notes all day. What was the teacher doing? How were the students reacting? This teacher gave the kids pieces of paper where there were pictures of fruit or other items and they had to draw a line to the correct number. This was work for a child in kindergarten, not the third grade. This wasn't interactive at all. At one point, my son said that his neck hurt from looking down at this paper all day. There were no breaks. No subject changes. Just busy work. I didn't see the benefit of these self-contained classes. There was no learning going on. There was no curriculum. Just coloring. No instruction. Just outlining. I took so many notes that I had a very big binder that included daily observations from the class. Neither the school nor district didn't like that.

Another thing that the school did not like was that I would take Elvan out of school everyday at 12noon. The rule book said that students must stay in school for at least four hours per day to be considered present. After those 4-5 hours past each day, I said, "Elvan, let's go."

They would call me and say, "you can't do that. You can't remove your son from the classroom at 12noon." I reminded them of what their rule book stated and they didn't like their rules being thrown back into their face. So they questioned me as to why I removed him every day.

Why did they do that? Out comes my binder with days of notes and observations....

1. He is not learning.
2. It's not curriculum based.

3. There are no instructions.
   Do I need to keep going?

4. He is not being challenged.

5. All he is doing is coloring and tracing letters all day.

6. And the list goes on and on...

And this is the third grade? I requested for him to be returned to regular classroom learning. They rejected that request because I signed some papers. I didn't realize that the state and the school get more money for a child that is placed in special education. They also said that Elvan could not return to regular classroom learning because the district psychologist diagnosed Elvan with being borderline mentally retarded. I hired and paid for three licensed, educational psychologists to test my son. They were Dr. William Hellams (Columbia, SC), Dr. William Posey (Columbia, SC), and Dr. Frank Brown (Florence, SC). All of them performed 2-3 hour evaluations, as opposed to the 20 minute evaluation from the school district psychologist. After all three evaluations, they determined that Elvan was not retarded.

All three of the doctor's concluded that Elvan had high functioning autism. Some refer to it as
Asperger. This was a huge blow to me. It was almost like someone saying I had cancer. I was devastated. I cried for

days and weeks on end. My son has autism? I could depend on the results of these independent doctors because all of them said the same thing. My son has autism. What is autism? I called another meeting with the school district. I advised them that my son does not have ADHD as they erroneously diagnosed. Based on their error, I requested that my son be placed in the regular classroom setting. That request was still denied. I contacted educational attorney, Attorney Donald Gist for assistance. I also wrote a letter to the State Superintendent. At the time, it was Inez Tennenbaum. I believed that my son was being denied his rights to be in regular classroom and I asked Superintendent Tennenbaum how she would feel if her son or daughter was denied access into USC or Clemson for an unjustified reason to be subjected to a different school. As a parent, it didn't feel good to be forced to abide by rules that you don't agree with. I felt like this was an educational intervention. Especially after three medical professionals conducted testing and came up with the same conclusions that debunked the diagnosed of the district psychologist.

Now, in the third grade, my son needs an IEP and a parallel professional, also known as a shadower. They fought me on this until my lawyer, Attorney Gist got involved. That's when their tone changed. That when they suggested for us to meet. Now, let's talk about it. Let's negotiate. They agreed to put him in Arts and Craft and Social Studies.

"Are you happy now? We've put him in two regular classes."
That was their appeal.

My response was, "No! I want him out of self-contained."

The battle was hard. There were many prayers and many sleepless nights. There were days that I would park my car in front of the school and just cry and pray until the school day was over so I could see my son. I would ask God, "why? Why God? Why?"

God responded clearly to me and said, "why not? I gave this angel to you, for you to be his voice. Soon, you will see that you will be the voice of many children."

After my lawyer got involved, we had a meeting that settled the dust and brought resolve. They questioned where I wanted to Elvan to go to school. The school that I had to drive Elvan to was a good distance from my house and he wasn't zoned to that school. I told them that I wanted Elvan to go to the school that he was zoned for. That following Monday, Elvan was able to return to regular classroom learning at the school that he was zoned for. While Elvan was in the self-contained classroom, he didn't learn anything and I had to make another hard decision. The teacher said that he passed at the end of the school year, but I wanted him to repeat the third grade because I didn't feel like he was ready for the fourth grade. That was my decision and I signed papers to confirm the decision.

CHAPTER TWO

Elementary School

2

Elementary School

I want to begin this chapter by saying, "you must be careful of what you sign" and "you can't believe everything 'they' say". OK. Let's dive a little deeper.

When the school district psychologist tested Elvan and deemed to be borderline retarded, which was false, they had me sign a document to remove Elvan from regular classrooms. They wanted to assign him to self-contained classrooms. This was based on his cognitive level and their diagnosis, which was unsubstantiated. Being the analytical person that I am, I wanted to know the difference between regular classrooms and self-contained classrooms. "They" said that the self-contained classrooms were similar to regular classrooms and that the only difference was that the information was taught at a slower pace. Same curriculum. Slower pace. In that moment and based on their explanation, I was fine with it. So, I signed the documents. I was nervous about signing the papers, but all I could hear was that it was the same as the regular classrooms, but at a slower pace. I felt like I was doing something wrong. I felt like a young mother that couldn't raise their child on their own for whatever reason and had to put their child up for adoption. It felt like I was giving my child over to another set of parents that could possibly provide a better life for my child. I was really upset and for some reason, I couldn't shake the attached emotions and feelings. That said, I had to see how things were going to go in the self-contained classroom for myself. I went to class with Elvan every day. The more I went, the more I wanted to remove Elvan from that environment. The more I went and observed the daily activities in that classroom, the more I realized, I signed the wrong paper.

In this classroom, there was no effective instructions. There was no curriculum outside of busy work. Nothing was being done to provoke my son to want to learn. This was the third grade. My son had already passed Kindergarten through second in regular classrooms and now he was repeating the same lower-level work in this slower paced, self-contained classroom in the third grade. They did this busy work, went to lunch, went to recess and returned to this classroom to repeat it all over again. I gave the teacher an opportunity to prove me wrong. I was hoping things were going to change.

I gave it about 3-4 weeks after taking notes in a large three ring binder. Nothing changed.

Round One

I went to the school's resource teacher and advised her that I made a mistake. I want Elvan removed from the self-contained class. She advised me that I already signed Elvan over and it doesn't work like that.

"What do you mean? Elvan is my son!", I replied.

The school said that I needed to leave the classroom because I had observed enough. From there, I started removing Elvan from the classroom around 12:30pm daily. Based on the district handbook, he only needed to be in class for four hours in order to be considered present for the day. Like clockwork, I showed up and signed him out. There were days when I would simply stay in the parking lot and wait for 12:30pm to hit so I could sign him out. Why not? He wasn't learning anything, anyway. They didn't like that.

Round Two

I begged and pleaded with the school and the district to remove Elvan from the self-contained classroom. They threatened to report me to DSS and even have me disciplined for truancy. They didn't like that. I kept calling for IEP meetings with the school. They consistently replied that my request was denied. It was like Elvan was doing a bid in an educational prison.

Well, if they won't listen to me, maybe they will listen to the voice of the public media. I went on several radio stations to voice my opinion and extend my voice as a concerned parent that only wanted what was best for my child. While I was speaking up for my child, the school and the district was continually saying, "no, no., no!" Radio didn't work and that made me frustrated. So, I moved on to phase two: pickets. Do you remember how people picketed in peaceful demonstration for what they believed? I did the same thing. I, along with about 5 other people, picketed the school and the district for the sake of my son. They didn't like that. This made them angry and furious. One of the board members came out to the picket line and said that I was being foolish, ignorant and every other name that they could gather outside of my birth name, Florene. This was all because I was fighting for my son.

After some time, they came out to make an agreement with me. They started making offers.

"How would you feel if we allowed Elvan to take regular classes for arts, or music or social studies?"

How would I feel? How would I feel? This is the best way that I can describe their offer. How would a slave feel if they said we're gonna let you out of the master's house if you will work in the field a few days and also come back to cook the master's food and clean the master's clothes? Who wants to be a part time slave? No one wants that. I wanted my son to attend regular classes in their entirety and throughout the day. Partial freedom is not complete freedom at all.

Their response was, "that's not going to happen. You don't want to cooperate."

I felt angry., I felt hurt. I was so upset. I felt like they were holding my son as a prisoner. I felt like I had no voice. I felt caged in. I felt unheard. All I wanted was for my son to be educated according to the guidelines of the district's handbook. I guess my son didn't have the same rights as other children. The diagnosis from their psychologist was illegitimate based on their 15-minute examination and as compared to the thorough evaluation from three unbiased, licensed psychologists. My son convincingly passed kindergarten through the second grade with no problems.

Round Three

The school and district suggested that I stopped picketing

and making a public spectacle of myself. So, I hired an educational attorney. His name was Donald Gist. This was not a cheap undertaking. Getting legal representation for this type of ordeal was a costly affair that I didn't have the money for. I had to solicit funds from my uncle in Fayetteville, NC. Attorney Gist notified the district's attorney that he was representing Elvan and myself. He demanded them to stop sending me letters to stop picketing and making complaints about Elvan's self-contained classroom experiences. They were writing and corresponding with me as if I was a criminal.

My attorney scheduled multiple meetings over a couple of weeks. These were big meetings. Elvan had no clue of what I was going through just to protect his rights to receive quality education. I could see if he had been in regular classrooms and failed, but they had never given him a chance. Waiting for the results of these meetings were the worst. One of the final meetings included my attorney, their team of attorneys, and a few of my family members. After about 20 minutes, they decided to allow Elvan to attend regular classes, but they wanted him to stay at their school. I did not want him to continue at that school. I requested for him to go back to his zoned school, because they knew Elvan better and provide more assistance.

In my mind, I'm thinking that the fight was over. Yes it did, but the war had just begun. During all of the chaos of this school and fighting for his rights, Elvan wasn't doing well. He was performing to the best of his ability. He wasn't communicating with the other children. It wasn't until Elvan was properly diagnosed as having autism did the light come on. I began to study autism. Elvan was on a higher spectrum.

This is why he laid on the floor and listen to the floor as if sounds were coming out of the floor. This is why he always closed doors, cabinets, and dresser drawers. He couldn't stand for anything to be out of order. This is why he couldn't speak until he was three years old. This is why Elvan didn't give anyone eye contact. When he spoke to people, it was indirectly as if he was talking to the side of your face. He is autistic. Elvan suffered from a lot of sensitive stuff. He couldn't touch uncooked rice. His foot couldn't touch grass. When rain touched his skin, it made him cry. Elvan went through alot of things that met the criteria of what all three doctors said he had - autism. Now I know. This is what we're dealing with. How did I feel with the diagnosis of autism? I felt sad. I felt very sad. I knew this was a lifetime struggle. I felt like he would never be able to do things like other little boys. Oh my goodness. My son has autism. If I'm going to continue to fight for him, I must understand everything about autism.

I began my journey of studying the ins and outs of autism. The ramifications and the signs. What he needs. What he doesn't need. He's back in regular classrooms at his original school. Some of the teachers did not want to follow the IEP. These are requirements for my son's education.

"Here comes Dr. Fulks! She's a strong advocate for her son. Why do we have to make this accommodation? Why do we have to do this modification?"
So, now, the fight wasn't only with the district. The fight was also in the classroom.

I can remember two very influential people at this school. One was a teacher by the name of Ms. Jones. I believe that she fell from heaven. I think she was a designated angel for my son. Another person was the principal, Mr. Brown. He was a very understanding and compassionate person. The other teachers were something else. Elvan made good grades, but I decided to leave him in the third grade because too much had been going on and he wasn't ready for the fourth grade. So, I had to fight again and sign documents just to retain my son. I thought that this was best for my son.

The next year, he was placed back in the third grade. There were some battles with some of the teachers. They didn't want to comply, but they had no choice with an IEP in place. Some of the kids were fighting and hitting Elvan so he was assigned a shadower. This shadower was provided at the suggestion of the three doctors that I acquired for educational evaluations. At the beginning of each school year, I had a meeting with everyone that would be responsible for the education of my son during that school year. This included the para-professional, speech therapist, occupational therapist, and teachers. Lotty dotty! I met with everybody!

This happened every year until he graduated. Every summer, right before school started, I would call the school and schedule a meeting with all of the teachers and outline my expectations for everyone that would be working with me. This was an annual ritual that caused my anxiety to rise higher and higher. There was always someone at the school that refused to follow the IEP, Individual Educational Plan. As a mother, I had to remind them every year. I am not the student, but I am the voice of the student named Elvan.

> I am not the student, but I am his voice.

If you do not provide it for him, we are going to have a problem. The IEP is a federal educational law. It's just like a prescription. When Elvan had seizures as a baby, they give him the phenobarbital twice a day. He didn't like it, but it was necessary for grand mal seizures. You have to take the same approach with IEP's. This was a requirement of the school for my son.

Fulks Fact

It is imperative that you study and know the IEP for your child. You must know the accommodations and modifications for your child and you have to make sure that they are followed. If and when you see that the IEP is not being adhered to, please mother, father, guardian, called an IEP meeting with the team of individuals that are responsible for your child's education. If you don't do this, your child will be lost in the system.

Now, it's time for the fourth grade. Because we moved, to another neighborhood, Elvan had to change schools. This was a very prominent school in the same district, but the results of Elvan's education were not favorable. Elvan was flunking everything. I didn't get it. At the previous school, he was passing. When I spoke with the teacher, their only response was that Elvan didn't pass the test. Ok. Did you follow the IEP? Did you consult with the paraprofessional, his shadower. Their response was not satisfactory.

"I gave the information to Elvan's shadower. I don't know why the shadower didn't give it to Elvan."

Once again, we are embarking upon another fight. Clearly,

I was being targeted as the enemy again. Let me help you understand something else. Many times, the school doesn't realize that they are hurting the child when they target the parent that is fighting for the child. They thought that because Elvan wasn't passing his classes, that it would hurt me. No, that hurts my son and that causes me to fight harder. The main reason is because I know that Elvan knows his work. *School doesn't end at the ringing of the final school bell.* There are some parents that choose to further enrich the educational lives of their children after they get home. We'll talk about that later.

I am a woman of faith and highly favored by God. You may have kicked me out of the classroom because I observed too much, but that doesn't mean that I'm clueless to what is going on in the classroom. God always has a way of providing the necessary information from the needed individual that will give me further insight into the classroom. There was a Caucasian woman that worked at the school. One day, she came up to me and asked for my phone number. For whatever reason, I gave it to her and she said that she was going to call me. As promised, she called me and gave me some shocking details.

She said, "Mrs. Fulks, Elvan is being mistreated in this school. I have to visit classes for my other students and when I visit, Elvan is always sitting in the back of the classroom. I thought this was fairly off because Elvan is different. I even asked him why he wasn't participating and he said that they didn't want him too. I never heard the teacher encourage Elvan or ask him to participate. The teacher only mentioned that she didn't want to be bothered so she left Elvan in the back of the classroom. I think you should look into this."

All of this is going on while the other students are highly engaged throughout the classroom: looking at maps, observing animals, reading books. By now, my pressure is rising.

She goes further to say that the other students want Elvan to participate by asking him questions to engage him but the teacher, once again, told the class to leave him alone in the back of the classroom because he's not able to do what they are doing.

Hold your horses! There's more......
The woman had so much more to tell me. She said that she observes her students in that class while they are outside playing. While the other students are outside playing group games, Elvan is on the bench shivering in the cold weather. She asked the teacher, "why is that young man not playing and where is his jacket?"

The teacher said, "he must've forgotten it." When it was

offered to go into the class to retrieve it for Elvan, that was discouraged by the remark, "No. We'll be going in soon. He'll be ok."

Are you kidding me? I really wish I was making this up but this information was freely given to me by a concerned teacher. Here's my conclusion. They didn't hate Elvan. They hated me and they thought that they were hurting me by depriving my son. No ma'am. That doesn't hurt me but it does give me more reason to fight. My voice was too strong. My voice was too loud. My voice was too passionate. They failed to realize the level of servitude behind all of this work. While they tried to punish my son behind my back, I continued to serve as an advocate for my son and they didn't understand the God that I served.

If you're keeping up, I guess this is about Round Five or Six by now.

The Caucasian woman said that she loved all children and this was her only job. She asked me to not give her name when I reported these incidents. I gave her my word. I didn't even go to the principal. I went straight to the district office. The district office contacted the principal and called a meeting. In the meeting, the teacher denied everything. I threatened to bring in the informant, but I didn't want to break my word. Then, I told her everything Elvan said about his classroom experience. Elvan said that he sits in the back when you know he should be in the front of the class. These are the things that I had to put up with on an annual basis and this was just the fourth grade.

"What can we do for you? How can we fix this?", they said.

I want him back at the other school. The school where they take their time and follow the IEP as outlined. I knew that he wasn't zoned for that school since we moved. There was also no bus to pick him up for school. I didn't care. I had two cars in my driveway. He will get to school. I followed up that suggestion with a stern warning. If he can't go back to the other school, I'll be talking to every news outlet, radio and TV station to share about how this school district is treating this African-American autistic boy. You already know I can. You know I've done it before. Lastly, I have the ability to do it again. Needless to say, Elvan was able to go back to the other school, and his educational records beat him there by the next morning.

Let's pause for a quick second. For those of you that are reading this book and you know me personally, you already know that I want in multiple capacities. I want you to know that I was an emotional wreck in this meeting. I didn't enter as Dr. Fulks, even though I had enough educational credentials. I didn't enter as Pastor Fulks, even though

I always have a word in my heart to share. I entered as the parent and voice of Elvan. I can't promise that I used all of the best and polite words, because I was in a fight for my son's educational rights in the face of deliberate mistreatment. I have already asked God for forgiveness. In that same moment, I did transition from the parent to the Pastor. I shared with the teacher one of God's oldest principles as taught in Galatians 6:7.

"...whatsoever a man soweth, that shall he also reap."
Galatians 6:7 KJV

Furthermore, I explained to her that she infringed upon an innocent child and the Bible says that *"as you have done it to one of the least of these, My brothers, you have done it to Me".* **Matthew 25:40 KJV**

I felt sorry for that teacher, but I knew her day was coming. I got Elvan's backpack and left that meeting.

These are the types of frustrations, moments of anger and sadness that I had to take home. This had a traumatic effect on my son. I can remember one night when Elvan was having a hard time going to sleep. He was frustrated as to why the teacher hated him. I kept telling Elvan to please go to sleep because he had to get up early in the morning to go to school. He was thinking about things he could do for the teacher to make her like him. "Mom, can you get her an apple or a picture of an apple? Teachers like apples and that will make her like me."

I questioned Elvan. "Why do you think that she doesn't like you?" Remember, this was the school that I requested to go back to.

Elvan replied, "I don't think she likes me because she pushed me and I almost hit the floor."
In my mind, I'm confused. Why would she push my son? So, I asked the questions to Elvan because that type of action is inexcusable. "Why did she push you?"

"She pushed me when I tried to hug her."

It took everything in me to not cry in front of my son. It took the hand of God to cover my eyes and stop the tears from flowing down my face. With the help of a woman's intuition and a mother's creativity, I had to ease the mind of my son so he could go to sleep peacefully for the night. I acted as if I called the teacher. I had no clue about that teacher's home phone number.

"Mrs. Teacher. How are you? I'm calling for Elvan. He thinks you are angry at him because he tried to hug you. Ok. I'm tell him. Elvan, she's not angry at you. She forgives you and she loves you. Do you forgive her?"

Elvan brightened up and said, "yes, Mom" and he fell asleep right away. Guess who didn't go to sleep at all that night?

Ding – Ding – Ding

Round Seven

From 10pm the night before until the next morning, I was sitting up, fully dressed in my business attire, but once again, it's time for war. This is another example of the pettiness and foolishness that I have to endure when the accommodations and modifications of Elvan's IEP are not followed. This same teacher has been reported before how not following the IEP. Now, she chose to take the frustrations out on my son. That next morning, I walked Elvan into the school and into his classroom as normal.

"Good Morning, Elvan", said the teacher.

"Good Morning", said Elvan.

I instructed Elvan, "Elvan, do not go anywhere. Please stand beside me."

I got directly in the face of the teacher with my Austin Reed business suit. I was so close that I could have kissed her. This was intentional because I wanted her to hear me clearly.

"Did you push my son because he hugged you?"

"What are you talking about?", she replied.

I repeated, "Did you push my son because he hugged you?"

Then, her memory came back. "Oh! Students aren't allowed to hug teachers because it can be viewed as sexual harassment."

Are you kidding me? Elvan is a very affectionate child. He's in the fourth grade. He wouldn't sexually harass you.

"Well, he's a big boy and he felt like hugging me. So, I gave him a little push.", said the teacher.

Game, Set and Match! I'm glad you admitted it. By this time, the principal was coming down the hallway because he thought a fight was about to happen. I kept my composure. I wasn't going to push her. I did let the principal know that his co-worker just admitted to physically putting her hands on my son. There were multiple ways that she could have handled this situation.

1. She could have advised Elvan to have a seat. Thank him for the hug, but explain that we don't hug in

school.
2. Explain why we don't hug in school.
3. Call his mother so I can explain #1 and #2

I'll be the first to let you know that #3 wasn't going to happen because of the self-proclaimed vendetta that the teacher had for me. My explanation would have been clean and straight to the point in a method that I knew my son would have understood. Elvan, don't hug her anymore. She doesn't like that. Stop hugging her.

Rather than take the peaceful route, you chose to respond in a manner that you thought I wouldn't find out. He didn't get injured because there was a desk behind him that held him up and kept him from hitting the floor. To me, that was a hard push because Elvan isn't a small boy. She started crying. Tears don't move me. I told the principal to handle his teacher and that I was going to the district office. After I left the district office, I was going to the file an assault report with the Sheriff's Department because she put her hands on my son. As I was leaving, the principal was running me down.

"Dr. Fulks! Please, can we talk about this before you move forward?"

We went into his office. I didn't file charges and I didn't

call the cops. I just wanted an apology from the teacher to me and my son. I also wanted this notated in her record as a teacher. I've always shown mercy on some of these teachers. She didn't want to follow the IEP. These kids are different. These kids can learn, but they all learn differently. As a certified teacher, they have to realize the importance of following the accommodations and modifications of each student's IEP.

CHAPTER THREE
Middle School

3

Middle School

Prior to Elvan going to middle school, he had a very influential teacher that made a great impact on his life. His name was Keith Alexander. He was a male, African-American teacher that taught math. The fascinating thing about Mr. Alexander was that he understood Elvan's based on his own childhood. Because of that, he took the time to use his knowledge, love and patience to teach my different child that happened to have autism. It wasn't even about the learning disability. That didn't matter. It took patience because all children can learn. They just learn differently.

Elementary school ended and we entered the 6th grade of middle school. As normal, I met with the entire instruction team that was going to be assigned to Elvan during the school year. I didn't have any issues until the middle of the semester.

Guess what? It wasn't because of anything that I did. No picketing. No radio or TV interviews. No issues. I was called to the school because one of the teachers wanted to meet with me about Elvan. OK. Maybe this is a concerned teacher wanting to discuss his progress and opportunities for growth. I entered the meeting and the teacher addressed how she felt uncomfortable with Elvan because he kept telling her that he liked her nail polish.

Did I hear this teacher correctly? Did you read that correctly?

I was called into a meeting away from my busy life schedule based on a teacher's lack of comfort because my son said her nail polish was nice. She said that was a form of sexual harassment. My son gets bullied without retaliating and not fighting back but this teacher thought that she was a prime candidate to get sexually assaulted by my son? She tried to redact her comment by saying she was just comfortable. I suggested that she get a new job because my son wasn't going anywhere. Later, I found out that this teacher was uncomfortable with Elvan across the board. Nope! He's not leaving the classroom. You leave! Every year, I had to deal with the accommodations and modifications of Elvan's IEP. Now, I had to deal with a teacher that was uncomfortable around this big, African-American student that only offered you a compliment. You're intimidated by compliments? She could have called me and made me aware. I would have told Elvan to not say it anymore and the issue would have been resolved. Here's the root of the problem. He's black and you're white. Elvan told most of his teachers that he didn't like black girls and that he liked white girls. Most of the white girls that Elvan was attracted to were beautiful. However, this teacher was a sight for sore eyes. That's the best I can put it and that alone should assure that teacher that she was safe.

I always taught Elvan to not hit girls. I just don't believe in men putting their hands on women. There was this one instance when Elvan was being repeated kicked by a female student. It got so bad that he came home with scratches and bruises on his legs. Now, this has to stop. I gave him permission. When you go to school tomorrow, kick her back. As a parent, you never want your words or lessons to be thrown back in your face, but here it goes. "Momma, she's a girl. You told me not to hit girls."

"Hit her back. This is too much.", I replied. He would not hit her back. The next day, he came home crying because the girl kicked him again. This little girl was sneaking. Whenever Elvan's paraprofessional would leave the room, the little girl would go over and kick Elvan. I told the principal that we needed to have an IEP meeting. In the meeting, I advised them about the situation, and I told them that the bullying had to stop. If she kicks him again, I am going to call the cops and she will be hauled off to juvenile detention. Please tell her parents what I said. Ultimately, they moved the girl away from Elvan.

Next was the seventh grade. There's an old song that said, "More Money – More Problem". If I had to write a song, it would be "More School – More Problems" or "New Year – New Problems". Every year, there was a problem that had to be addressed at the school. Mind you, this is a new school. This is the seventh grade. Elvan is a big guy. School started around August or September. This didn't start until October or November. For some reason, Elvan started coming in the bed to sleep with me and husband. That was strange, but something scared him. He was actually terrorized to put it lightly. On top of that, he started wetting the bed. Big boy. Seventh grade. Wetting the bed. Now, I know something is going on. I asked all of his teachers if someone was bullying him. Anytime we talked about going to school, he would get really quiet. Then, over a length of several nights, he would wake up crying. So we talked about it.

"Mommy, I don't want to be gay."

My ear must be playing tricks on me. "Say what, Elvan?" He was an upset mess.

"I don't want to be gay, Mommy!"

"You're not gay, Elvan."

Since the school didn't know what was going on, I took Elvan to a child psychologist. After two or three treatments, the psychologist told me that Elvan was sexually molested. Elvan knew the name of the student and the exact date that it happened. On that particular day, Elvan's paraprofessional had a mild heart attack and was out for a few days. The school's resource teacher was supposed to tell the replacement for that day all about Elvan's accommodations and modifications. They did not do that. One of Elvan's accommodation requirements was for him to not go to the restroom with supervision. This was because he was picked on and bullied so often. They failed to fulfill this accommodation on this day. Elvan was sexually molested by another boy on this day. He wasn't penetrated but the boy performed oral sex on Elvan. This confused Elvan because the other boy said, "now we are friends and this is what friends do for each other. Aren't we friends?"

Elvan answered slowly, "um, yeah." Nothing else happened because Elvan wanted to get back to class. Once again, I had to go to the district office. I advised them that they needed to pay for Elvan's therapy because he was traumatized by this event as a result of the school not following the details, accommodations and modifications in Elvan's IEP.

Everything points back to the IEP (Individual Education Plan). The key word is "individual". In this case and every case throughout this book, the individual is Elvan. Not the parent. The child. The student. There is an outlined plan for the child's/student's education that must be adhered to in order for the child/student to be positioned for success in their educational success.

The school dropped the ball. They didn't follow the IEP that clearly states that Elvan is not to go to the restroom alone. The school's rebuttal was that "this allegedly happened." Allegedly? Are you serious? Allegedly? Elvan urinated on himself in front of his peers because he feared going to the restroom again. And you say allegedly? I noticed a change in my son and my son questions his sexual orientation because of a situation that you say "allegedly" happened. I wrote a letter to the state's Superintendent of Education addressing my concerns. I sought compensation for my son's therapy from the school district due to their lack of compliance to my son's IEP. At this time, the state superintendent was different and we all met with their legal representation. They weren't going to argue with a parent that was not at fault. They agreed with the majority to pay for the therapy. They asked for the name of the doctor where Elvan would receive this therapy. They agreed to pay for all therapy sessions until Elvan was healed of this trauma. I could have easily sued the school and the school district for this mistake on their part. However, my primary goal and the purpose of my fight was for my son to receive the proper education and instruction to receive a high school state diploma. I was wrapped up, tied up, and tangled up in my son's education. I was fully engulfed in it. I didn't want my son to receive a certificate of completion. I wanted him to receive an accredited high school diploma as conferred by the state. If I wasn't preaching the gospel as a Pastor, I was focused on Elvan and his homework, his classwork, his medication, and everything he needed. This was my entire life. That was the seventh grade.

Elvan is a big guy. I didn't put him into football or basketball. Elvan wanted to play music. He is very musically inclined. We considered placing him in band. The instructor went to the principal of the middle school and said that Elvan couldn't be in band because band was as competitive as football and basketball. The straw that broke this camel's back was when the band director said that he didn't have time to provide extra attention and instruction for Elvan to learn trumpet. He was more concerned about winning championship for the band. Elvan was hurt and disappointed. I could have demanded the school to get a separate music teacher to teach Elvan so that Elvan could participate in the band program, but my attention was more focused on Elvan's academics, curriculum, and the achievement of receiving his high school diploma. You must use wisdom as a parent and know which battles to choose and fight. I chose to hire a piano teacher for Elvan and he picked up that skill fairly quickly.

Let's move on to the eighth grade. We moved again, so Elvan had to go to another middle school. The principal was nice. The teachers were nice. I went through the same beginning of the year ritual. We had an IEP meeting and everything was going good until the end of the year.

Fulks Parental Fact

Remember, when you are the voice for your autistic child, there will always be a fight.

At the end of the eighth grade in middle school, you have to prepare for IEP on the high school level. We had a meeting with the upcoming high school, the school district and all of the teachers that would be assigned to Elvan. The first thing that the district worker said was, "you're going to release the shadower from Elvan, right?"

What? Why would I do that? The district worker said that this was the ninth grade and they didn't want to have a stigma placed on Elvan. I questioned if they knew the purpose of a shadower and why Elvan had one in the first place. You have to make sure that the individuals for the next school are well learned about the history of the student and why certain accommodations and modifications are in place for the student. The incoming staff and faculty members for the high school didn't do their homework. They didn't know anything about the student. They didn't know anything about Elvan's accommodations and modifications. They didn't know anything about Elvan and the first comment was that he wouldn't need a shadower in the high school. Why wouldn't he? Have you read his file? Don't you know about the bullying? Did you read about the molestation? Clearly not. So as a parent, I had to teach the teacher about what they could have read and reviewed on their own time. This is why my son needs a paraprofessional.

This person tried to further convince me that my son wouldn't need a shadower. Meeting over! I walked out of that meeting and went directly to the district and spoke with the Superintendent. When we spoke, I told her to never send that worker to my son's IEP meeting ever again. The Superintendent tried to advise me that she was the transitional person for student's that would go from the eighth grade to the ninth grade. Her purpose was to help students transition from middle school to high school.

My response was, "let's talk about transition and more specifically, my son's transition from middle school to high school. First of all, that district will be a part of the son's IEP meetings. Secondly, every accommodation and modification from my son's current IEP will transition to high school. The shadower will continue in high school. Lastly, this isn't because I said so, but because the law says so."

Fulks Parental Fact

Individual Education Plans transfer with the child throughout their educational careers: elementary school, middle school, high school and even college.

My son's educational ability, mental capacity and behavior dictated that he still needed a shadower. He didn't stop having autism because he went to high school. Your child's disability didn't stop. So why should their accommodations and modifications stop? As your child matriculates through school, it is our hope that their cognitive skills are fine-tuned so that they can function clearer as they get older. In order to assure and assess their ability, a shadower/paraprofessional is necessary.

Please let me help you understand why a shadower is necessary. Elvan is a very inquisitive person. He always knew that he was different, but he didn't always understand the differences. I had to explain to Elvan why he had someone shadowing him at school.

Do you remember when you got lost down while walking through the hallways at school and no one could find you?

That's why you need a shadower.

Do you remember when some of the students wanted to fight you because you were snitching and telling the teacher everything they were doing?

That's why you need a shadower.

Do you remember when you left the classroom and went outside to wonder in the grass and no one knew where you went?

That's why you need a shadower.

Lastly, do you remember the many times that you didn't bring your books, homework or chrome book home?

The purpose of the shadower/paraprofessional is to keep the student focused and on task. The shadower's job was to come to my car upon pickup to tell me Elvan's homework so I can keep Elvan accountable.

That's why you need a shadower.

Elvan has an understanding that I am here to help him. Even in church, Elvan always says that he thanks God for being here and that he thanks his mother for always fighting for him. He has never forgotten that. He knows that I will be his voice as long as I am here in this Earth.

Seeing Elvan graduate from elementary and middle school gave me a high level of satisfaction and gratification. He even received some certificate for A and B Honor Roll in Science and Social Studies. The thing that gave me the most gratification was when teachers and administrators approached me to say, "if all parents were like you and took the time to take ownership of their child's education, school would be a better place."

I'm thinking to myself, "aren't all parents like this?" Later, I found out. All parents don't have the same level of concern and care for their child's education. I was dedicated to being a voice and advocate for my son. One of my good friends and partners in Elvan's Lifeline, Diane C. Gaines, acknowledged that I was doing a lot for Elvan during elementary and middle. She advised me to save my strength and energy. Her specific words were, "you may have won the fight, but now, you must prepare for the war." They did not want Elvan to graduate high school and I was about to enter one of the hardest fights of my life.

INTERLUDE

Emotions Of A Concerned Parent

Interlude

Emotions Of A Concerned Parent

Many times, throughout the pursuit of education for disabled children, the parents get lost in the shuffle. I want to be the first to tell you that your emotions matter and that you are not forgotten in the complexities of these battles. I wanted to take a moment right here to explain how I felt as the parent during some of the most traumatic ordeals for my son.

When Elvan was molested in the restroom during his seventh-grade year, I was an emotional wreck. As parent, you trust that your child will be protected while attending school and outside of your attentive care. IEP's are in place to outline special provisions for your child while they are in school. Even after the school paid for Elvan to attend therapy sessions and counseling, I was afraid to send him to school. Trust goes a long way and throughout his educational career, I lost trust in the education system. However, I still remained in the fight. I was willing to go on the battlefield every day. I was willing to take on whatever challenges that presented to me. I prayed many nights as to when this fight would be over. I knew it wouldn't be over until he graduated.

When I sent Elvan to school now, my mind rambled through a full gambit of thoughts. What was Elvan doing? Is he alone? Is someone touching him inappropriately? Would he know what to do if they do do it? Even if everyone was having a great day, my life was completely miserable. My ultimate goal was to get Elvan to graduate. The endgame was to get a high school diploma.

What do I do? Do I send him to school, or do I homeschool him? Should I put him in school to get the necessary stimulation and interaction with his peers. Autistic children need that type of interaction.

All I knew to do was pray.

God, I need you in this moment.
I need you to dispatch angels to cover my son throughout the day at school.
I pray that he feels comfortable in that environment, and I pray that the classrooms, teachers, faculty and staff members
create an atmosphere that is conducive for learning.
In Jesus' name, Amen.

The band situation placed a sour taste in my mouth. While I could have fought to have Elvan participate in band, it wasn't my battle fight. I consider how beneficial the band environment could have been for Elvan. He could have been one of the best trombone players in the world. I believe that all children with disabilities should be afforded the same opportunities as children without disabilities. Some schools and teachers discredit the abilities of autistic children and check out before the child has had an opportunity to check in.

I live in a capital, metropolitan city. Prior to moving to this city, my son attended school and participated in regular education classroom settings. We didn't know what was going on with him completely, but we knew he was different. Elvan was making A's and B' effortlessly. He had no problems. Initially, he was diagnosed as being ADHD. He was smart, but he learned differently. When we came to this new school district, he was quickly diagnosed as borderline, mentally retarded. They wanted to immediately banish him to self-contained classes. I didn't think that was right since he was passing classes.

After establishing his IEP and having the assistance of a paraprofessional, Elvan got on task and was more focused. The next hurdle was in the transition to high school. This is where we are now. I was warned by my good friend, Diane Gaines, to prepare for high school because it was going to be a fight on another level.

The final IEP meeting of Elvan's eighth grade year was a preparation meeting for high school. During that meeting, I had so many obstacles and challenges placed in front of me and I refused to buckle under pressure. First, they said he would have to be in another self-contained classroom. Then, they said that he wouldn't have a shadower. Then, they wanted to recommend him for an autistic program where he would clean up around the school and cafeteria and basically learn housekeeping and chores. I can teach my son how to clean up and fold his clothes at home. Finally, they wanted me to choose which track I wanted Elvan on. Track? Elvan's isn't going to run track? Sarcastically, I knew what they meant by track but I was just playing into their hands. They said that they would offer Elvan a vocational track, career track or state issued, high school diploma track.

BINGO! That's the one. I want Elvan on the state issued, high school diploma track! That was my plan the entire time. I wanted my son to get the same education as everyone else and receive his high school diploma. Then, here comes their sarcasm. "Well, you know. If he is to get his state issued, high school diploma, he has to pass the Exit Exam." By this time, I was done with this meeting. I knew that Elvan didn't perform well on standardized tests. I gathered my items. I told them that Elvan will be in regular education classrooms in high school and at the conclusion of high school, he will receive his state issued, high school diploma without taking the exit exam. The school psychologist questioned me. "How do you think your son is going to get a high school diploma without taking and passing the required exit exam?"

I confidently told her that she does not understand or know the God that I serve. The one who sits high and looks low. "Just watch!" And I walked out of the meeting.

CHAPTER FOUR

High School And Graduation

4

High School And Graduation

It's a new year! It's a new school!

The routine and the plan stay the same. We have our beginning of the year IEP meeting as requested by me and arranged by the principal. This meeting includes everyone that will contribute to the education of my son.

> Parents: This should be part of your plan annually. It sets the tone for your child's educational success.

All of the teachers joined the meeting: English, Science, Social Studies, Math and the paraprofessional. I didn't want to have a repeat of anything from elementary or middle school. We planned for success. Because of the trauma associated with my son being molested in the seventh grade, I required, as part of my son's accommodations, that there be a substitute shadower in place in the event that the current or scheduled shadower is out for the day. If one can't be assigned, I would just come and pick up Elvan for the day. I couldn't afford for my son to be misplaced or forgotten for any amount of time during the day. That left too much room for error. Needless to say, I never had a problem with Elvan being molested again.

Change is not always good. For my son, he stressed over change. He was in a new school with new teachers, new faces and new challenges. Plus, this was a huge school.

"Elvan, are you okay? Are you excited?"

"No ma'am. I'm nervous. I'm afraid. I'm afraid that I won't fit in they won't like me."

I had to encourage Elvan that he is a handsome young man. He was dressed up and had on nice shoes. I dressed Elvan in the best because he was a representation of the best, the kingdom of God. I needed him to feel confident in himself and I wanted him to make a great impression on his teachers and classmates. On his first day at the new school, Elvan asked me if I could stay with him. That was the hardest "no" that I ever had to give him. All I could do was tell him to go with his shadower and he would be ok. In the back of my mind, I knew he was scared. I dropped him off and went back to my car and cried. I wanted Elvan to be more independent as a ninth grader. Ninth grade went okay outside of some challenges in Algebra One. He had a great Algebra teacher and he made it through.

Tenth grade presented more challenges. The classes were harder and they were more challenging. If there was a problem, a meeting was called and the issue was resolved immediately. While I didn't have to battle with teachers in the ninth grade, there was one teacher in the tenth grade that simply didn't want to follow the IEP. Elvan was taking US History, Algebra Two and Psychology. I don't know why they signed Elvan up for Psychology. This specific teacher did not want to follow the IEP.

"I'm not going to chop up this work. You said you wanted him in regular education classes. If you wanted someone to chop up the work, you should have put him in autistic classes. I'm not going to break down the curriculum for one student. The other students don't get that."

These are the words from that teacher. I found fallacy in multiple areas of her unproven premise. First of all, the IEP says to break down the curriculum. You must adhere to the IEP. Secondly, my son is not the other kids. My son is different and you have no choice but to teach him differently. She was trying to assign 85 questions to my son. That's too much for anyone in one sitting. After a certain amount of questions, students with disabilities will shut down. They feel defeated. Their self-esteem gets low. Once again, I had to call an IEP because there is evidently a disconnect between the teacher, her responsibilities and the details of my son's IEP. In this same class, Elvan received three F's on three tests in the same week. Three tests. Same week.

"Mrs. Teacher, why was Elvan given three tests in the same week when his IEP requires him to receive a period of three days with a study guide before each test."

She replied, "Well, I did read that. I give pop up quizzes and I don't think it is fair for him to receive more time than the other students."

"Ma'am? Who are you? You are not exempt from following the IEP!" I was flabbergasted by her response. This same teacher would give out homework that involved taking close to 25 page of notes from the textbook. Children without disabilities have an issue with that so I knew Elvan wasn't going to be able to do it. I'll be the first to admit that I crossed the line in this homework assignment. When Elvan began complaining about his hands hurting due to writing so much, I did the homework for him. When Elvan returned home with that assignment's grade is was a "0" because it was not done in Elvan's handwriting. I pleaded with the teacher unsuccessfully for my son because he was in pain trying to complete the assignment. She would not budge. After further conversation, she gave Elvan more time to complete the assignment which was aligned with the accommodation of his IEP in the first place. IEP's make life so much easier.

These are the types of battles that you have to fight when dealing with certified nuts, I mean teachers that don't care to follow the IEP. I never said that Elvan could not do the work. I wanted to bring to her attention that if she is going to assign such a large volume of work that it would need to be broken down as outlined in the IEP. The only reason that she decided to finally follow the IEP was when I threatened to contact the State Board of Education. Elvan finally got out of her class with a final grade of D+. The only thing that matters is that he passed.

The battles and fights of the tenth grade continued. I wanted Elvan to take virtual classes over the summer like Physical Education, US History and Statistics/Problematics. Elvan didn't do well with running up and down bleachers and other physically strenuous activities. They thought that Elvan would do better in those classes while amongst his peers. Well, that rule should apply across the board. Why are there athletes that are allowed to take virtual classes over the summer? You don't know if they are actually taking the classes. I was going to send Elvan to a certified teacher to make sure that he got the work done. I operate with a high level of accountability and honesty. I wanted to do things the right way. I had to pay for a certified teacher out of my pocket. I didn't know anything about Statistics and Problematics. Elvan and his certified provided video proof that he could do the physical activities or other classroom work over the summer for the virtual classes. This wasn't always required of the nearly 1,000 other students taking virtual classes, but we had to fight. At the end of the summer, he passed, and we got the victory. Now, we prepared for the 11th grade.

Somewhere between the tenth and eleventh grade, the state decided to remove the exit exam as a requirement for students to graduate from high school.

Let that sink in. During Elvan's transition meeting from middle school to high school, they doubted me when I told them that Elvan wasn't going to have to take the exit exam in order to graduate. I told them in that meeting, before walking out, "you don't know the God that I serve." Trust me when I say, "Only God Can Do It!"

In the 11th grade, I only had one issue with the school. They wanted to run an updated psychological test on Elvan. Mind you, in their first psychological test which only lasted

15 minutes, they determined that Elvan was borderline, mentally retarded. Based on the test of three additional, certified psychologist, it was further proved that Elvan was autistic, not borderline, mentally retarded. I declined their test. Why would I allow your unproven testing method to cast another false report on my son? You can't even give my son a vocabulary test. Declined. Declined. Declined! Eleventh grade went well after that.

Now the 12th grade? The 12th grade was the best year of Elvan's educational career. Elvan was passing classes. Elvan was making friends. Because Elvan had so many credits, he was given early dismissal which meant that he could get out shortly after 1pm. Oh! He thought he was really something leaving early while others had to stay for the entire day. I shed a lot of tears in the 12th grade. It wasn't because of my need to fight, but it was because the fight was finally coming to and end. Elvan had more than enough credits to receive a state issued high school diploma. I asked the Superintendent if I could sit on the floor during the graduation. Elvan had an assigned teacher to walk with him during the marching processional. I sat with the teachers and administrators so I could be close. I cried the entire graduation. No. Like for real. While the Pomp and Circumstance was playing, I was crying. During the speeches, I was crying. When Elvan crossed that stage, I was crying. When the band was playing and the soloist was singing, I cried the entire time. Do you understand the years of fighting and battling that I had to do for my son? This was the culmination of some hard work on my part and on the behalf of my son. These were not only tears of joy, but they were tears of relief. The fight was over.

This was such a momentous occasion that the local news stations and newspapers featured Elvan on TV, and on the front page of the newspaper. On the day after the graduation, we received so many phone calls and messages commending Elvan on a job well done.

Elvan wasn't ADHD as initially diagnosed. Elvan wasn't borderline, mentally retarded as falsely diagnosed. Elvan Hanley learned differently as a successful, autistic child. Elvan received his state issued, high school diploma by completing all of the requirements with a 3.4 GPA.

CHAPTER FIVE

Finding Employment

5

Finding Employment

When Elvan graduated from high school, I grieved. I wasn't sad, but I was fatigued from so much hard work. I allowed Elvan to also rest for three months before making his next life decision. He could have attended the University of South Carolina to major in Music, but he said he was tired of school. Guess what? I was tired of school too.

I really want to convey to all of the readers of this book as to why I grieved for three months. Fighting for Elvan for all of those years was like dealing with a terminal disease. Everyone thought I would lose. I just kept on fighting. They threw every obstacle and challenge in my direction. I kept on fighting. I cried through Elvan's graduation because it was the end. The fight was over. It was the death of the hard-fought battle. I don't remember a lot of the good times. Elvan went to his high school and I can't remember the details of that joyous occasion because I was still in the fight. He was a showstopper at that prom. But what do I do now? Elvan's education engulfed my entire life. I couldn't really enjoy my life because I was advocating for his life. Every day was filled with, "get up Elvan", "you have homework Elvan", "you have a test coming up Elvan", and "you can do it Elvan". There's a story in the Bible that talks about David being very distressed by everything that he had going on. That's exactly how I felt. The key to that biblical story was that after all David had been through, he found enough energy to encourage himself.

> *"And David was greatly distressed; for the people spake of stoning him, because the soul of all the people was grieved, every man for his sons and for his daughters: but David encouraged himself in the Lord his God."*
> **1 Samuel 30:6 KJV**

I didn't have a lot of people patting me on my back. I didn't have a corner, like a boxer, where I could be rejuvenated or reenergized. I had to encourage myself to keep pushing, keep going and keep fighting. You must prepare your child for life and that is also, life after Mom is gone. This is a must.

Now, we needed to plan for Elvan's future. Elvan needed to enter into the workforce. The TV show, 60 Minutes, categorized this population of people as cliffhangers. They were individuals that were done with high school and entering into adulthood. What do they do? What do we do with them? Where do they go? How do they transition into the workforce? The reason that I wanted to find Elvan a job was fueled by the fact that he couldn't be under me all day at home. He had to find something to do. Cliffhangers stay at home in their rooms all day. They play video games all day. It is imperative for parents to find something for their child to do because one day, I'm not going to be here. That's a hard pill to swallow, but it is reality, and you have to prepare your child for it.

I tried my best to get Elvan into the workforce. This was a challenging feat until I had a dream. I dreamed that Elvan was working in the Kroger's Grocery Store. I followed that dream into an actual Kroger's. I explained to the manager that my son needed a job and that he was autistic. While seeking employment for your child, you have to be upfront about everything and explain the tendency of your child. Your child simply wants to work. He/She isn't there to hurt anyone. By securing a job, it gives them an opportunity to interact with others and build their interpersonal skills. Kroger's has been a tremendous blessing to my son during the first years of his employment. Elvan has worked for Kroger's since 2016 and he is still there. Kroger's assisted in changing the entire trajectory of my son's life.

Graduating and finding employment for my son wasn't the end of our story. I have a burning desire inside of me to help as many parents and children with disabilities to achieve more in life. I feel like a modern-day Harriett Tubman. Now, that Elvan was freed from the harsh grip and restraints of the educational system, I wanted to make sure that future parents and children didn't go through the same things that I went through. To house the great vision and purpose of my efforts, I formed a 501c3, non-profit organization called Elvan's LifeLine.

CHAPTER SIX

What They Never Told Me

6

What They Never Told Me

There are a lot of things that every parent must be taught concerning the educational system for children with disabilities. At one point during Elvan's educational career, they wanted him to be in self-contained classes. By now, you know that I fought against that and eventually, he was allowed to return to regular classrooms. The first that they never told me was that in self-contained classrooms, the classes will not count towards or prepare him for high school. That meant that all of the time in a self-contained classroom would not count toward a state issued high school diploma. To me, and on behalf of my son, that was a waste of time. In order to get a high school diploma, you must have completed Math, English, Science, and Social Studies. There are more extracurricular classes that go towards the required 125 credit hours. If your child is in a self-contained classroom setting, the hours do not count.

Self-contained classrooms in elementary and middle school do not prepare students for high school. For example, basis math is taught in elementary and middle school. That won't prepare your child for Algebra, Geometry and Trigonometry in high school. The same applies to English classes. Dr. Seuss and Charlie Brown are not going to prepare your child for Hamlet, MacBeth and other Shakespeare works. It is impossible to expect a child to learn on that level when they have not been prepared for that level. Self-contained classrooms are glorified day cares for older children. Based on all of my studies and observations, there is no curriculum or opportunity for learning. I was not told about the results of self-contained classrooms versus regular education classrooms. I had to find out for myself and with the help of my good friend, Diane C. Gaines from Orlando, Florida.

If your child goes through all of their schooling, they will only be given a Certificate of Completion or a Vocational Certificate. This goes back to those "tracks" they offered my son. They offered vocational, tracks, career tracks, or a high school diploma. You know which one I chose. You can't do anything with a Certificate of Completion. You can't apply or be admitted to any university, college or technical school.

To my understanding, you can't get into college or the

military without a high school diploma. I want to encourage all parents. If your child has the cognitive ability and skill to enter and participate in regular education classrooms, get them in there.

You must commit yourself to your child's educational career. Just because the bell rings at the end of the school day, doesn't mean that the school day is over. As a parent, you have to dedicate extra time in making sure that everything your child has learned during the day is being retained. That may mean that you have to tutor your child. In most cases, parents do not have the time or energy to tutor their child after working a full day. In that case, you must consider hiring a tutor. After school programs are not recommended in this situation because children in after school programs are not always focused on doing homework and that could be a distraction to your child that needs the extra time to learn. Yes, it will cost money, but it will be worth it. Tutors specialize in subject matters that can be further enriched after the school day is over. They can make sure that your child is actually learning during the day and then make sure that homework is completed before the next school day. This is also an opportunity for your child to get a head start on future lessons. This is a win-win situation.

With Elvan, I refused to have him limited to self-contained classrooms. I didn't see the benefit in having him in there.

Once he was allowed to return to regular classrooms, he had to repeat the third grade. He wasn't prepared in self-contained classrooms, so I wasn't going to allow him to move forward yet. Just because your child leaves the confines of a self-contained classrooms, doesn't mean that the disability goes away. Elvan was still autistic. He had the same symptoms. He was still on the same spectrum of autism and when he got into the regular classroom, he got the same homework as all the other students. That's the only area where you child and the students in that class are similar. Your child has the assistance of a shadower and an IEP that outlines what you child can and cannot do along with the expectations for when it can be done. The Individual Education Plan is structured, designed and developed to accommodate that child's learning disability.

When the final school bell rings, the school day continues for most children with disabilities. Other children have extracurricular activities such as cheerleading and sports. Children with disabilities can't always do that. Elvan has always been a fairly big kid. Coaches from multiple sports teams wanted Elvan to play for them, but I had to decline the offer because education was the more important thing for Elvan. Sports would take up a lot of time after school when that time was better used for learning. Elvan will not be playing football. In the tenth grade, the wrestling coach wanted to try Elvan out for the wrestling team. I told the coach that Elvan wasn't going to be on the team. He tried Elvan out anyway.

"Elvan, do not let me take you down on the mat", the coach said.

"What do you mean?", Elvan inquired.

The coach said, "I'm going to try to take you down on the mat. Don't let me."

In less than three seconds, Elvan reversed the coach's move and had the coach down on the mat. Now, the coach really wanted him on the team and my answer was still no. The goal was to get Elvan a state issued high school diploma. That's it and that's all. Anything else would have been a distraction. Do you know why I fought so hard? "They" (and there were a lot of "they") told me that he would never get his diploma. I'm the type of mother that steps up to a challenge because I have something deep down on the inside that makes me want to persevere. When they say no, I say yes. If they say that it can't happen, I say it will happen. When they said that Elvan would have to take the exit exam to graduate, I said that he wouldn't and by the time Elvan was preparing to graduate, the exit exam had been removed from the requirements. I spoke with confidence and I spoke that into existence. They don't know the God that I serve. I knew that God was gonna work it out and I knew that God was gonna work in Elvan's favor.

Parents, you have to be an intentional voice in your child's life. Every year, I stuck with the same routine. By doing this, it showed the teachers, the administrators, the schools and the district that I was serious about my son's education. I felt like it was me against the world and in this case, the entire school district. Let me help you to understand. It's not your child that they are against. It's your voice. Your tenacity. Your perseverance. Your determination.

Opposition and second opinions came from every side. Every year that I went through this routine, I had to deal with teachers, principals and administrators. Do you know who the hardest opinion came from? Not a teacher. Not a principal. Not a district administrator. The hardest opinion came from my mother, Mary Ann Riley. She has since gone on to Heaven. She suggested that I just let Elvan go into the autistic classroom. She said to me, "Florene, you are going to kill yourself fighting for Elvan." Normally, I listen to my mother, but I was dedicated to the mission. After all, I couldn't trust the district based on their invalid results.

Parents, if you have the ability, get a second, third, or fourth opinion. Don't allow anyone to wrongfully categorize your child. Early on in the process, I decided that if Elvan didn't learn in the regular education classroom, I would let him go to the self-contained classroom. Elvan got in that regular classroom and dispelled all rumors. He learned. He learned differently, but he learned.

CHAPTER SEVEN

My Prayer, God's Response

7

My Prayer, God's Response

As a minister of the gospel for over 40 years, I often ask God why. I've had visions of my son going to soccer practice or football games, with of course, my son being the star player. I never imagined having a son that would not understand the strategy or game play of football. I questioned God a lot. Why can't I send my son to the store to pick up a loaf of bread without being bullied or misunderstood by a store clerk or a cashier? When my son met pretty girls, he would introduce himself in this way. "Hi! My name is Elvan and I like girls. Being autistic, he has no social understanding. I told Elvan many times, "when you meet a pretty girl, you don't say that. Just say, Hi! My name is Elvan." As an innocent 15-year-old, he did not understand that. I'm almost certain with everything that's in me, if I had lived back in the 50s, or 60s, Elvan would have been another Emmett Till.

There were many days, upon dropping Elvan off to school, that I would park in the school parking lot and just cry. This was my prayer.

My Prayer
God, why?
What have I done wrong?
Why is this battle placed upon me?

God responded just like this.

God's Response
Why not you?
I equipped you to fight this battle.
This battle is bigger than you and this battle greater than Elvan.
You will help thousands of parents who have asked or are currently asking me the same question.
You will show them how to fight and to be the voice of their child.

Immediately, I stopped crying. My answer to His response was, Yes Lord. I will do it. I drove to McDonald's and had a cup of coffee. Did I park my car again. Yes! Did I cry again? I sure did. Did I ask God why again? Definitely not! I knew from that one conversation with God that I was a chosen vessel to speak for children that were in similar situations as my son, or maybe even worse. The frustration was still there. The pain of fighting for Elvan's rights to education was still there.

Prayer is simply communication with God. That means that there is dialogue, not monologue. It's not just your words and requests to God. If you take the time to listen, he will speak to you. In this moment of inquiry, I could have asked God why and had a pity party. However, I was in a vulnerable position wherein I needed God to help me. God's response was specifically for me. He provided the answer that I needed.

CHAPTER EIGHT

Preparing Your Child For Next (Life Without Mom)

8

Preparing Your Child For Next
(Life Without Mom)

One of the biggest questions that I've always asked myself was "what would happen when I die?" Elvan has plenty of uncles that love him. He has a sister, Imani, that adores him. There is no one, absolutely no one, like your mother. Who's gonna fight for my son now when I die? I hear that question a lot of from parents that have children that depend on them.

Social skills for autistic children can vary based on the spectrum level, but communication is going to be essential to their life. Here are some tips to prepare your child for life without Mom.

You must do things to prepare, not just yourself, but them for life without you. Prepare your child educationally to graduate from high school, college or technical school. Then, train them in a trade or skill area.

Do not be satisfied with a disability check.

Make them as independent as possible.

Teach them basic directional activities such as how to get home.
If there is a car accident and I am unconscious, how do they communicate with the police.

They should be able to communicate their home address and phone number.

If they are being abused, they should be able to communicate this information to the proper authorities.

I'm sure that one day, Elvan will want to drive. He can be properly taught that skill. I don't fear Elvan driving. I fear how he will respond to a police if he gets pulled over. Furthermore, I fear if the police will respond correctly to an autistic citizen. I fear receiving a phone call that my son was resisting arrest and the police shot/killed him.

Parents, and more specifically mothers, you won't be there forever. You must equip your child for life without you.

Parents should get legal guardianship for their son or daughter. Furthermore, you should secure co-guardianship in the event that you are not there. This person will be able to assist with making sound decisions such as surgery, getting married and moving away from home. You need someone that can make the hard decisions. Would you allow your autistic son to get married and move across the country away from family? That answer is probably no because you want them close to family.

My mother, Elvan's grandmother, passed away when Elvan was around 16 or 17 years old. He had a hard time with that. I explained to him at that same time that I was also going to die one day. He told me, "if you die, I'm gonna die too". I told Elvan that we are not joined at the hip. He said, "No! If you die, I will find a way to die too even if I have to look it up on Google. I want to be with you in Heaven." I told Elvan that he can't do that. Talking to a 16-year-old autistic child is like talking to a 9 or 10 year. While he didn't understand it then, he understands now. He has a sister, a stepdad, cousins, and a lot of aunts and uncles that love him and will take care of him. His understanding in that moment was that wherever his mother was, he wanted to be there too. That comment from Elvan kept me up for several nights. I was devastated for multiple reasons. First, he considered dying. Secondly, he was not prepared for life without me. Now, he understands. I let him go to sleepovers with family members. I encourage parents to not hold their disabled child too close. That's not good for their personal growth.

Everyone child is not like my child. Your child may not be able to have a job. If not, put them in a day program where they can learn how to live among other people. They can do activities to further enhance their cognitive and critical thinking skills.

I've always assured Elvan that even if he can't see me, I am always in his heart. You have to prepare your child for your absence. I teach Elvan social skills and how to interact with other people. That's why he has a job. Kroger's has been one of the best things to ever happen to Elvan. Disability checks will not meet the needs of an adult. Because Elvan works, the check is even smaller. Some people advised me to take Elvan off of his job to get more disability. I was not in favor of that advice. Elvan works so that he can improve his social, interpersonal and interaction skills with his peers. I don't want Elvan isolated in his room all day. I don't want him to stay home all day. I want Elvan to experience the best that life has to offer for him.

You have to prepare your child your life without you. I

can't say this enough. I want to commend every parent of a disabled child. You've done a wonderful job in raising them. You've done a great job in parenting them. Now, do an even better job by teaching them how to navigate through life without you.

CHAPTER NINE

No Not One

9

No Not One

As the mother of an autistic child, one of the most difficult things to navigate through, outside of the educational process, is the need to find extracurricular activities during the summer months for my son. It is very difficult for him to understand team play, group strategies and basic peer-to-peer activities due to his spectrum designation and social delay. Physical sports such as football, baseball, basketball, and soccer are not the norm. A child such as mine would possibly score for the other team. It was always hard to get Elvan into physical recreational activities. It was also hard to find programs and activities at local recreational facilities for disabled children.

Once, I had a conversation with a city official. He suggested for me to take my son to a local YMCA or to a local parks and recreation facility. I have to draw the picture like this.

As a 9, 10, or 11 year old child with autism, Elvan would not be able to handle himself freely in one of those facilities. Elvan can't swim, but if invited to get in the pool by his peers, Elvan would, unknowingly and without reservation, jump into the pool. He would not think about his safety due to his excitement to be included in fun activities and the open gesture of friendship. Elvan would jump in the pool without considering that he can't swim. Elvan is a big boy. Elvan would drown.

I proposed for the city to create a recreational facility for disabled children. They need an outlet just like other youth and children. In some cases, youth and children with disabilities have to drive miles away for recreational activities that are catered to them. Social development is essential for disabled children, especially those with autism. It is not fair that they don't have anywhere to go. Team sports are excellent for creating friendships but when you are a child with autism, you are picked on, bullied and not picked for team activities. Most parents leave their children at home for this reason. Elvan gravitated towards music because that was his passion. He loved playing the piano and I invested in that passion for some time, but he needed peer interaction and physical exercise.

As a tax paying citizen, like many other parents, I thought that a recreational facility for disabled children would be beneficial for that population, but there was not one. This facility could employ workers that specialized in caring for disabled children. They would know how to respond in the face of a crisis. They would understand what a specific child was going through. They would understand the child's strengths and weaknesses.

Elvan and I have a friend named Dr. Mobley. Dr. Mobley has a son named Brandon. Brandon asked the same questions as Elvan. Where are my friends? Why doesn't anyone like me? Why can't I go to the movies with my friends? They crave social interaction just like everybody else. Why not have a facility that caters to their needs?

In the area where I live and through my city, there are on average 2-3 recreational facilities for the youth, but no, not one for children with disabilities. I believe that needs to be seriously considered. There is an old, abandoned movie theater in my city that has been available for years. It is ideal for a facility that could house sports activities, movies, computers and video games for disabled children. This isn't just in my city and local area. This is happening everywhere. Can we get just one? One facility. One location for our children. No one wants to send their child away over the summer. There are camps in Atlanta. There are camps in Arizona, but that is too far away. We want something here that we can send our children to for a couple of hours without worrying about their safety.

I speak to parents all of the time about what their disabled child is doing. Most are in their bedrooms all day. Elvan plays video games all of the time. Elvan has every video game system and so many games. All he does is sit in his bedroom and play games all day. That's one of the reasons why his eyes are so bad. He can't do anything without his glasses. If we keep our children in their bedrooms all day, they will become depressed, anxious, angry, violent, and ultimately, what we dread the most – suicidal. Yep! Suicidal. They feel alone, ostracized, and like no one loves them. Well, take them to church. Church? That's only 1-2 times per week. What about the rest of the week? If there was a facility for disabled children operated by the city like they do for non-disabled children, they would have an outlet.

But there is not one. This is very disturbing to me. For those of you that are reading this book, look around your communities and neighborhood. Can you find one? Consult with your government officials and politicians. There should be funding and grants for this type of project. You can take an old building and revitalize it for this effort. Build it for these children. Having a facility of this caliber will benefit the personal growth and development of disabled children. They have a right to be exposed to fun, extracurricular activities. This can be a multi-purpose facility to teach trades and on the job training. This is important. If I ever get my hands on the type of money to make this dream a reality, I will build it.

I feel like every community should have a facility for disabled children. I searched all over and I couldn't find one. No, not one!

CHAPTER TEN

10 Things Every Parent Should Know About A Child With Learning Disabilities In The School

10

---

10 Things Every Parent Should Know About A Child With Learning Disabilities In The School

1.   It's YOUR Child, Not The School's

Always understand that while the school is responsible for providing and developing goals, accommodations, and modifications to your child's curriculum, it's the parent responsibility to ensure that those goals, accommodations, and modifications are carried out. You should learn your child's IEP and 504 like the back of your hand. Knowledge is power. Your power is decreased greatly if you don't study the laws of the IEP and your child's constitutional rights as it pertains to your child's disability. No one will do that for you. Don't come into an IEP meeting clueless. Know their language. Understand what they are saying. When I came to that realization, I studied the IDEA (Individual Disability Educational Act of Congress) laws and statutes like it was food for life and it was food. It was the necessary food for my child's educational success. You cannot depend on the school to do it all by themselves. It's YOUR child. Yes, you can obtain an advocate to work with you. Oftentimes, if you want true success, you will have to hire an educational attorney or a paid advocate that knows just as much or more as an educational attorney. In the beginning of my battle with the schools and the district, I hired an attorney. He was excellent and knowledgeable, but he was also expensive. I pondered to myself and reached the conclusion that I could equip myself with the same information to help Elvan. My brilliant sister, Diane Gaines, an educator of over 20 years, pushed me, taught me, and equipped me to become a monster in the IEP meetings (just kidding). Most of the time I'm pretty nice and calm. When I walk into the meeting, I know my information. Parents, it's YOUR child. Don't hold the schools responsible for everything.

2.   Know And Choose Your Battles

Understanding the target goal for your child is essential. I knew from the onset, after researching and medical doctor testing. My target goal was "GRADUATION WITH A HIGH

SCHOOL DIPLOMA". I let nothing stand in between Elvan and graduation. Absolutely nothing or nobody. When you come into an IEP/504 meeting, other subjects arise. Don't linger. Discuss them and move on. Some concerns will come up and you may feel like you want to call a meeting, or you may want to rush into the principal's office to rant about that issue. Don't do that. Think about it. Ask yourself the question. Is this really pertaining to my target goal? Will this make or break the plans for my child? If not, swallow your tension and dry your eyes. Move on. I recall once in the 7th grade, Elvan wanted to participate in Band. He always loved music and instruments. The first two weeks of band class, the band instructor called me into a meeting. Clearly, he didn't know that he was speaking to the "Harriet Tubman" for my son. I didn't play with any teachers or administrators that got on my last nerve in regard to my son. I sat there and listened to the band instructor, but yet the rattlesnake in me was ready to strike at any given time. He said "Elvan has autism right?" I didn't answer that question. I just said to him, "proceed". He then continued to say, "Band is so competitive. We often go and compete with other schools on various levels. I don't have time to sit with Elvan one on one to teach him the instrument that he chose. He appears that he can learn the instrument, but the amount of time that it would take, would slow me down from the entire class. You may want to consider removing him out of this class." I responded, "You may want to ask questions about me before calling me into a meeting and talking about you don't have time to work with my child". He continued to attempt to talk to me while I walked out of the meeting. Yes, while he was talking. I went straight to the principal's office and said to her, "it's not my problem if the school doesn't have a lower level, non-competitive band class. I'll fight, go on tv, radio and ask the public, 'do children with autism get to participate in band just like non-disabled children'?" That would have been my platform. In my normal fashion, I stormed out of the principal's office and got ready to gear up. When I got to my car, I put away that tough mommy face and allowed myself to cry and scream, for my son. Then, I considered, who should I go to first? My connection at the newspaper. My connection at the TV station. Or my connection at the radio station. Then, I heard God speak. He said, "none of them. This is not your battle. Remember, your goal is to get him out of high school. Being in the band has no barren on graduation." When I returned to his school the next day, I walked into the principal's office and said, "remove him out of band, and put him in arts and crafts." She did just that. I had to explain to Elvan in a way that he would understand and not feel hurt. Parents, choose your battles wisely. Every concern and issue is NOT A FIGHT!

3. You Must Apply A Stern And Sound Voice

You are your child's voice. I understood a long time ago

that I had to be the voice for my son. He was able to talk at the age of 3 where he could be understood. His comprehension of language was always a problem. When issues and concerns, regarding to my son's educational, medical or social needs arose, I spoke on his behalf. If you know that the teachers, or the school in general are saying that your child can't and you know your child can, then speak up. Ask questions. And yes, research their answers for validation. When my son was in the 3rd grade, a district psychologist tested my son using one of the intelligence exams. He said the test scored my son to be "borderline mentally retarded". I knew that wasn't true. I followed up those test results with examinations from three other outside psychologists. All three. I repeat all three said that he wasn't retarded. Retarded is such an ugly word to justify placement in self-contained classroom setting. All three outside psychologists said that my son had "High Functioning Autism", not borderline mental retardation". Since that day, I fought tooth and nail against anything the school district said about Elvan. If they were right about some issues, I put down the proverbial "boxing gloves". If I didn't agree, the fight was on. You are their voice. If you're not their voice, who is? No one loves your child as much as you. You are the one who nurses them back to health. You are their quiet place from a noisy world. You are their pillow to rest upon, when they are tired and frustrated. Therefore, you are the voice that fully understands that they have feelings and rights when they cannot express them. You have to be the one to do so. You must.

During one of my many IEP meetings, the occupational therapist gave me an idea about how Elvan interacts with others and respond to basic task. When all the kids went to wash their hands for lunch, Elvan would look at the soap and stand quietly at the sink. She would advise Elvan to get some soap and turn the water on. Elvan would just stand there looking at the soap dispenser and water faucet. She said, "Elvan doesn't know how to wash his hands."

Even as I write this and reflect on the event from 15 years ago, my eyes are full of tears and my heart is racing. I am sad. I yelled out in that meeting, "you are a bold-faced liar! My son knows how to wash his hands!" Later, I found out that the soap dispenser was more modern than Elvan was accustomed to and he was amazed by it. "Why didn't you help him with the new dispenser?"

The teacher replied, "all of the other students figured it out. Why couldn't Elvan?"

"Because my child isn't like your other students. He's different. He's autistic." This was the best response that I could give her.

Parents don't allow anyone to paint a picture as if your

child is stupid, ignorant and lacks basic learning skills. No, our children are not like other children. Be their voice and defend them at all costs.

4.   Attend All IEP And 504 Meetings. Stay Involved

It is imperative for parents to attend all meetings involving their child. Your child will have various IEP/504 meeting to develop his/her educational plan. Some of those meetings will be to add or subtract various information in the plan for your child. Whenever there is a meeting, you need to be in attendance. If I couldn't be at a particular meeting, I would have it cancelled and rescheduled. I never wanted anyone speaking on behalf of my child, in my absence. Parents have made me aware of decisions being made without their approval and in their absence. The schools and district will make vital decisions in your absence, especially if you never attend. It's your child. You must be there. Don't leave important educational decisions in the hands of the school. Don't be a "yes" parent by just nodding your head to everything that's being offered to you. While the IEP/504 meeting is taking place, the child remains in the classroom. If you are not careful, you will look up and your child will be in a 10th grade, self-contained high school classroom. The worst part about this is that none of the credits will qualify your child for state issued high school diploma. Instead, they will get a 12-year Certificate of Completion. It'll be too late for your adult temper tantrum. If you had attended the IEP/504 meetings, you would have known that every child must have 4 years of Math, English, Science and Social Studies inside of a regular education classroom to get a high school diploma. Follow your child's IEP/504 like the roadmap to graduation. It really is crucial.

5.   You Must Know And Fully Understand Your Child's "Complete" Disability

Accept the level of strengths and weaknesses in your child. A primary character of their child's disability, that every parent must be extremely knowledgeable in, is their level of strengths and weaknesses. It is so important to know what your child is good at. If your child is not good in math, they should only learn what is necessary for living. Do not put them in a class wherein they are not cognitively able to comprehend. That's like setting your child up for failure. Understanding what you child can and cannot do is essential. Adding stress on them can lead to mental complications such as anxiety or depression. Place more emphasis on their strengths. Allow them to see what they are good at and capitalize on those attributes. Do not advocate for your child to be in a gifted English class if there is a comprehension deficiency present. You must have adequate knowledge of your child's disability. I fully understood that my son had weaknesses in Math. I never selected an advanced Math class. I simply wanted a high school diploma for future endeavors. I never applied for my son to go to medical school or engineering schools/universities, because I knew that was out of his range. However, a high school diploma was not. Many said it was impossible, but I believed God and I knew that it was within my son's capabilities. He did it. He graduated with a 3.36 GPA. If your child cannot function in general education classes, then gather research from various specialists. If the specialists reach the same conclusion, then must accept that information to be true. It's not about you. It's all about your child. Every child should be loved and happy.

6.   Learn Your Child's IEP And 504 Plan Like The Bible

If your child is to ever succeed in school, with an IEP/504 plan, you have to know it like the Bible. Come into the meeting so prepared, that you don't need to see a copy of your child's plan. That will show the teachers and staff that you have studied it and know it. Have in mind target areas that you want to discuss. Yes, it is a team effort, but you hold the highest vote. They will preach to you that it's a team decision. You will hear that repeated over a hundred times. Clearly, in my case, everything was based on mom's approval. If my gut instinct said "no" then, it was a no go.

For example, when Elvan was in 10th grade, I was introduced to virtual high school classes. I knew for a fact that Elvan performed better with one-on-one instruction. However, even in general education classrooms, he received assistance, but not one-on-one. I signed him up for several virtual classes. The IEP Team boldly said "No". They suggested a larger classroom setting inside the school. I disagreed and wanted to try it. It was within my rights as the parent to do so. After going back and forth with the IEP team, I was able to sign him up. I hired a certified, seasoned, retired Math instructor and Elvan attended her private school for the summer. He successfully passed those virtual classes.

Parents, stand your ground. Know what is within the child's rights. If the football, baseball, and basketball players could take virtual classes, then my son can to. They weren't being questioned, so don't question me. My only goal was to help my son to receive a high school state diploma. It would not have been possible if I didn't study, research, and help develop my child's individual educational plan. You must do the same.

7.   Communicate With The Staff Members That Are Important To Your Child's Growth And Learning Progress

Effective communication is essential. Parents, please remember that all teachers and principals are not the same. There are some good and loving teachers in your child's school. Communicating with them in the right tone and during the right time is important. I am convinced that Elvan was taught by an angel for two years. I've never seen such love and patience like this 3rd grade teacher. You would have thought that Elvan was her flesh and blood. His 5th grade Math teacher also stood out. This Math teacher taught Elvan the fundamentals of Math with love and music. He reached my child.

Parents, don't walk around with a chip on your shoulders. Loosen up and allow people to help you and your child. I remember when Elvan was attending a new school in the district. One of the therapists dropped her phone number in my car as if it was a secret and asked me to call her immediately. She kept walking. I really didn't know what was going on. I called and she proceeded to tell me how Elvan was being mistreated and ignored by his teacher. The same teacher would tell the other children to leave Elvan to sit alone. Reflections to this interaction with the therapist makes me cry. The therapist begged me not to use her name, but she knew I would look into it. I never used her name. She complimented me on the love and passion that I used in fighting for my child. At the conclusion of that call, I never spoke to her again. That night, sleep could not be found. Needless to say, I walked in the school and informed the principal about what I was told. The principal wanted to have a meeting with that particular teacher. I said, "hell no! I want my son out of this school. There will be no meeting." I drove to district office and spoke to a few administrators. They said it was too late to transfer him to another school. I said, "Well, we will let the public decide." I then started calling all of my media contacts. Two days later, I got a phone call from the school district that the transfer was approved. People that don't care sicken me. I always had to do the most. If I didn't accept the fact that all school personnel were the same. I showed kindness to all the therapist and teachers and that's why she entrusted me with such vital information. It pays to communicate kindly with others.

8. Non-Disabled Children Have Rights Too

Parents of disabled kids may encounter some behavioral issues from their child in the form of hitting, kicking, throwing items, and loud interruptions. If you are the parent of such behavior exhibited by your child, then you must prepare for that child being removed from that classroom. Nondisabled children have the same rights to learn in a safe and non-threatening environment. Even though your child may be intellectually able to thrive academically in that general education classroom, behavior of a threatening interruptive nature will not be tolerated. You shouldn't expect it to be. You cannot expect other parents to understand that your child has a disability and to accept the spitting and hitting. If you were in their position, you wouldn't either. If your child can function and present safe social skills in the classroom, he will gain friends and playmates during recess. If not, your child cannot and will not be able to remain in general education settings. This is to ensure the safety of all students and that atmosphere is conducive for learning

9.   Prepare Before The School Year Begins

Throughout the summer and holiday months, school are always at the forefront of my priorities. Seasonal holidays, projects and papers were being prepared. You never want your child to fall behind in turning in projects and papers. Even though Elvan's accommodations gave him extra days to turn in those items, I always made sure Elvan had them completed close to the due date. This is crucial because: a) Elvan didn't understand that Christmas break was not really Christmas break for him, b) the slightest distraction would put him a week behind due date, c) I didn't want him to always stand out for being extra late and d) he needed to practice oral presentations of his projects over and over. There were times when his teachers would suggest that Elvan didn't have to orally present his project. I would always say, no thank you. He will do his very best and he always did well.

During the summer months, he was always placed in tutoring or summer school to maintain reading or comprehension skills. Never give too much space for failure. Besides, there are those who want your child to fail. When you constantly say my child will succeed, there's always an opposing force that will do everything it can to see that the success will not come. Two weeks before or after school starts for the fall, I always arranged informal IEP meetings to get acquainted with the team that would be working with my son for the current year. This meeting was also to go over Elvan's present accommodations and modifications as listed on his IEP. This was essential. I wanted to ensure that the entire team fully understood what I was expecting of them and what they were expecting of me. A few times, certain teachers would comment that they felt that some of Elvan's accommodations were unfair. I would always say, "I don't think that Elvan being diagnosed with Autism is fair, but these are the cards that life dealt me. And the meeting proceeded.

Plan For Success!

10. Search Out Support Agencies And Groups In Your Community

It really does take a village to raise a child. You cannot do it alone. Advocating for your child can get strenuous and disheartening. Talking and sharing with similar parents who have children with similar disabilities can be resourceful. Just listening to their struggles and triumphs can assist you with dealing with yours. Iron sharpens iron. Attending workshops and classes can help you to find ways to aid your child with various issues and concerns. I repeat. You cannot do it alone. Researching and asking questions will become your strongest asset. I linked up with Autism Society of Columbia, SC and they helped Elvan with various needs. They were a great support early in Elvan's middle school years. Do your research. There are many agencies that can and will help you and your child.

CHAPTER ELEVEN

Elvan's Lifeline (Non-Profit Organization)

11

Elvan's Lifeline (Non-Profit Organization)

After Elvan's graduation in 2016, I felt completely lost. Years of fighting and advocating for my son's education were over. Now what? My son's testimony of education success was felt by many people. My journey resounded to many parents, and they flooded my phone and inbox with cries for help with their learning-disabled child. Then, the light bulb came on.

Harriet Tubman traveled from slavery to freedom. Once she discovered the route to a better life, she lived a selfless life of sharing the information and freeing others. That story resonated with me. Now, I seek to provide the same assistance to thousands of families and children like my son. In 2017, my sister, Diane C. Gaines (Orlando, Florida), and I formed our 501c3, non-profit organization,

Elvan's Lifeline. The purpose of Elvan's Lifeline is to assist parents in developing IEP/504 plans and teaching them the significance of each. We seek to go into the IEP meetings as advocates for families and children and to support them throughout the process. Lorene Riley serves as our Administrative Research Assistant. We are a powerful team.

The name of our non-profit organization, Elvan's Lifeline, is derived from the fact that the Individual Educational Act of Congress law saved Elvan's education from not failing. These laws are just amazing. We will continue to work with parents and students, to ensure success and that every child will be educated in the least restricted environment as possible.

For More Information About Elvan's Lifeline

Email:
revflo@hotmail.com

Write:
Elvan's Lifeline
4145 Hardscrabble Road
Columbia, South Carolina 29223

Donations Can Be Mailed To:
Elvan's Lifeline
4145 Hardscrabble Road
Columbia, South Carolina 29223

Donations Can Be Sent Via CashApp To:
$PraiseHim2021

All donations will be allocated towards research,
equipment and books for our families and children

About the Author

Dr. F. A. Fulks

Dr. Florene Fulks is the Pastor of Only God's Word Christian Church. She has been preaching the Gospel for over 40 years. Dr. Fulks received her Bachelor's Degree from Benedict College (Columbia, SC), Masters Degree from New York University, Masters in Marriage Counseling from Dessault University and a Doctorate Degree in Religion Theology with an emphasis on Christian and Marriage Counseling from Overcoming Faith Bible College. She is the proud owner of Quitting Is Not An Option, also known as QINO, a family and marriage counseling service. Dr. Fulks is a well experienced, licensed marriage counselor with over 28 years of service. In 2017, Dr. Florene Fulks created Elvan's Lifeline, a registered, 501c3 non-profit organization that assists families of children with learning disabilities.

Dr. Florene Fulks is a proud member of the Delta Sigma Theta sorority. She's a sister and friend. She is the loving wife of Jacobs Fulks. Together, they have four beautiful adult children.

Dr. Florene Fulks is the epitome of servanthood and an

example of Harriet Tubman's perseverance and tenacity. Her life's mantra is "If I can help somebody, as I travel along the way, then my living shall not be in vain."

For Disability Consultations and Speaking Engagements,
please contact
Laronda Kennedy - Administrative Assistant
803.908.6943

Resources

www.mayoclinic.org

Autism Society of Columbia, SC

Holy Bible, King James Version